PRIMA DONNA

AN OPERA
IN ONE ACT

Libretto by

CEDRIC CLIFFE

Music by

ARTHUR BENJAMIN

Vocal Score

BOOSEY & HAWKES

AN IMAGEM COMPANY

DISTRIBUTED BY

HAL•LEONARD®
CORPORATION

7777 W. BLUEMOUND RD. P.O. BOX 13819 MILWAUKEE, WI 53213

CHARACTERS

FLORINDO ..	.. *A Venetian Gentleman* ..	.. Baritone
ALCINO ..	.. *His friend*	.. Tenor
THE COUNT ..	.. *Florindo's Uncle* ..	Bass-Baritone
OLIMPIA } FIAMMETTA } ..	.. *Of the Opera Chorus*	Coloratura Sopranos
BELLINA	*Florindo's Maid*	Light Mezzo-Soprano
A PASTRYCOOK & HIS ASSISTANTS FURNITURE REMOVERS TWO NEGRO PAGES }	.. .. ..	Mute persons

Time. Middle XVIII Century

Scene: A room in Florindo's house in Venice. Doors R and L. At back, a recessed balcony giving on to the Canal. This can be covered by a curtain, which is open at the beginning. At either side of this, at the back, two cabinets, which can communicate with each other across the balcony. They each have double doors opening into the room. These are of grained glass, so that when the lights are on in the cabinets and off in the main room, the occupants of the cabinets cast a clear silhouette on the doors. The room is unfurnished except for one or two plain chairs and two plain tables with pen and ink on them.

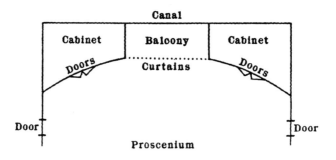

PRIMA DONNA
An Opera in One Act

Libretto by
CEDRIC CLIFFE

Music by
ARTHUR BENJAMIN

B.H. B.K. 692

Printed in U.S.A.

2

H. 14184

6

coun - try I see lit - tle else but vege - tab - les, And I do not find them ex-

poco rit. **Meno mosso**

- cit - ing. So when I come to Ven - ice I wish to be gay, have a

poco rit.

Fl.

fling once a - gain! Thank God and all the Saints I am not yet too

(spoken)
ALC:- Old Ruffian! FLOR:- Who? Me?
ALC:- No, fool! Your uncle! Go on.

old to en - joy a pret - ty face"

ev-er know *her* fav - ours last long-er than a man's mon-ey? She won't

colla voce

ALC. Oh! Oh! Oh!

look at me now.

W.W.

Poco lento

FLORINDO *with exaggerated despair*

The sun may shine, I have no eyes to see.

sempre arpeggiando

Cello Solo

espressivo

Women may smile, they will not smile on me. The Fates to some are

A7

12

H. 14184

LC. chance. But can O - lim-pia do it? Would not, perhaps, my lit-tle Fiam-

- met-ta do it bet-ter? She is at the Op - era too I'll wa-ger that

Più allegro

LC. she could wheedle money out of a Jew beg-gar!

LOR. No! No! No! No!

Allegretto poco ritenuto

ALC. *thoughtfully*

LOR. O - lim-pia is the best. *That* is settled. Oh!

rit. - - -

Obs.

FLOR. *(spoken)* Wait though. That solves one question. But how about the supper?

B *doubtfully*

LC. Oh, go to the Jews and ask them to help you for one last time.

LOR. Yes, it's the on-ly

Più mosso

Use the old man's name. Say that he can't last way.

LC. much longer. They'll fall at your feet when they know he's com-ing.

H. 14184

ALC. My dear Florindo, pull yourself together.
FLOR. All right. I'll write to Olimpia at once.
Then I'll go to the Jews and you go to
the Pastrycook's to order supper.

(dialogue during pause)

B1

FLORINDO
Yes,   it's the on - ly   way.   Bel - li - na!

lunga pausa He calls

hold chord during dialogue

(spoken)   BELLINA *enters*   BELLINA   Allegro vivo

I must write a note, too   To er my landlady   You called, Sir?

Bel - li - na!   Bel - li —   Yes.   Take this letter at

leggiero ma legato

p Clt. & pizz.

once   to Madam O - lim - pia   at the   Op - era.   It's ve-ry im-

rit. - - -

BELLINA
Ve-ry well, Sir.

-por-tant. There's a   du-cat for you if you're back in less than half an hour.

Hn.

Clt. Bsns.

H. 14184

18

H. 14184

Allegro

I know, I'll take them both. Then both ought to be sa-tis-fied.

Allegretto

(slyly innocent) To serve both God and Mam-mon They say is wrong. But

why? I think that's on-ly gam-mon, To serve both God and.... Mammon__ At

B5

least a girl can try! To see that nei-ther's

flout-ed, And not to fa-vour one, My du-ty stands un-doubt-ed To

TRIO

25

broiled meats, Sun-ny Ma-deir-a, ba-ron-i-al broiled meats, Sun-ny Ma-deir-a, ba- broiled meats, Sun-ny Ma-deir-a, ba-

Port, Brand-y by bum-pers and beer by the quart, Cham-pi-on -ron-i-al Port, Brand-y by bum-pers and beer by the quart, -ron-i-al Port, Brand-y by bum-pers and beer by the quart,

chee-ses, the fin-est of fish-es, Cham-pi-on chee-ses, the fin-est of fish-es, All..... Cham-pi-on chee-ses, the fin-est of fish-es, All.....

The Curtain falls to denote the lapse of one hour.

GAVOTTE

Brass

Woodwind

After the repeat the curtain rises. Ballet of furniture_
removers and pastry cooks. They fill the stage with rich
furniture, light candles and lay a sumptuous repast.
Musicians are seen
on the balcony.

C3

Curtain
Rises

(l.h.)

C4

Flutes

&c.

Pizzicato

cres -

Bsns.

MUSETTE

33

(Musicians on stage)

Alcino and Florindo enter.

Andante
ALCINO
You see, my friend, The fai-ry's wand is

Orchestra
delicato

waved; Dull lead is turned to gold! Fine

H. 14184

fa-brics and be-deck-ings gleam Where none was seen be - fore. Fine foods to

tempt you, Rich wines to de-light you, Sweet mu - sic to

melt you to thoughts of love! Thank your good fai-ry, friend, for

Più mosso

this.

FLORINDO

A fai-ry with a long, hooked nose Who'll come to me one day, With cries of

cres _ _ _ _ cen _

qual - i - ty more un - al - loyed, A fra - grance more en-

-tranc - ing to the sense, Than all its for-bears in the same high

do *f*

D2

rall. *pp*

line. The last long kiss when

pp Clt. Solo

molto *f ed appassionato* *sempre f*

two fond lovers part More deep - ly stirs the heart........... Than

molto *f* *sempre f*

all.............. the sur-feit that they once.... en - joyed.

Come Sopra

W.W.

pp

No mourning, then, my friend, for

rall..

pleasures that are past; But let's enjoy the rar - est of them all........ our

colla voce

Poco lento   **Allegro**

last!.......................

Clt.

Bellina runs in

p leggiero

40

H. 14184

44

H. 14184

QUARTETTE

Allegro molto

The Negro pages clap their hands over their ears and run out.

50

H. 14184

52

H. 14184

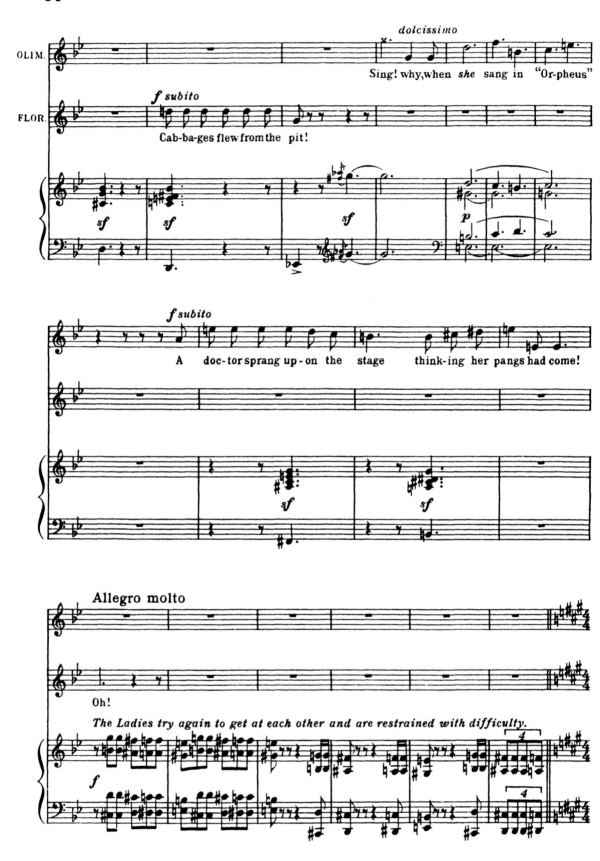

OLIM. *dolcissimo*
Sing! why, when *she* sang in "Or-pheus"

FLOR. *f subito*
Cab-ba-ges flew from the pit!

f subito
A doc-tor sprang up-on the stage think-ing her pangs had come!

Allegro molto

Oh!

The Ladies try again to get at each other and are restrained with difficulty.

56

H.14184

gon - do - la.......... to fetch and car - ry you, I'd ev - en, yes, I'd ev - en

Olimpia turns on Fiammetta.

And why not, Madam,

She laughs insultingly.

Ha-Ha-Ha- Ha-Ha- Ha! Ha-Ha! Ha - Ha!

mar - ry you!

pray?

The Ladies again try to attack each other.

61

62

H. 14134

UNT: Where........ is my ne-phew? Where is the boy?

Strgs. & Brass

rit. **Tempo meno mosso e molto giùsto** *The Count enters followed by Bellina*

Where is he? Ah!

pesante Vlns. Hns. *rit.*

LOR. Why Sir—

UNT: there you are, my boy! Did you get my let-ter?

ff p

Ad

Sir— Dear Sir, such a

Why d'you stand there gaping? Aren't you glad to see your old un-cle?

mp

Tempo giusto
They sit and pour wine

The wine is good, and good wine, Sir, is ne - ver un - time - ly. Ha - Ha - Ha - Ha! That's right my boy. Let's have an-o-ther glass.

ALCINO 1. A man may drink at twen-ty for rea-sons good and true; Be-

FLORINDO 2. A man may drink at for - ty for rea-sons good and true; Be-

-cause he has a thirst to quench— Be-cause he loves a heart-less wench— Be-

-cause he is at odds with life— Be-cause he has a nag-ging wife— Be-

-cause his blood is young and hot— Be-cause he's sick— Be-cause he's not. If

-cause he's rich, be-cause he's poor— Be-cause the wolf is at the door. If

these be not e-nough I'll name A do - zen more to you. Then

these be not e-nough I'll name A hun - dred more to you. Then

72

H. 14184

77

H. 14184

La Fi - lo - me - la!

The COUNT: *Two Filomelas, by Heaven?*
ALCINO: *(weakly)* Surely, Sir, there is only
one Filomela?
The COUNT: Two Filomelas—or am I seeing

80

H. 14184

SCENA

The two Ladies, accompanied by a Flute, Violin, Viola, 'Cello and Guitar (or Harp or Harpsichord) on the Stage, sing the Scena "Ariadne Desolate."

ADAGIO

Be6
OLIM.
FIAM.
ALC.
FLOR.
OUNT
ALCINO
FLORINDO
A - lone!
On
A - lone!....
Sh!
Sh!
Sh!
Sh!
pp
hear double!
Hear double!
ei - ther hand, on ei - ther hand The e - cho-ing rocks re - peat...... my moan. The
On ei - ther hand, on ei - ther hand The e - cho-ing rocks re - peat...... my
e - cho - ing...... rocks .... re - peat .... my moan.
moan...... The e - cho - ing........ rocks .... re - peat................. my
Fl.

Be8

ALC. *(stage whisper)* Indeed, it
becomes vastly exciting.

FLOR. *(stage whisper)* Be patient; it is
brighter in a moment.

It is almost more than I can bear.

H. 14184

Be10 *Fiammetta opens her mouth but no "E" comes.*

Molto allegro

ALLEGRO

kiss. Now sor-row melts to glad-ness Be-neath the God's fond kiss;

kiss. Now sor-row melts to glad-ness Be-neath the God's fond kiss; To

To Bac-chus and his mad-ness I yield my soul in bliss! To Bac-chus

Bac-chus and his mad-ness I yield my soul in bliss! To Bac-chus and his

and his mad-ness I yield my soul in bliss! My soul in........ bliss,

mad-ness I yield my soul in bliss My soul in........ bliss, me

my soul in........ bliss, I yield my soul in bliss, my soul in......

soul in........ bliss, I yield my soul in bliss, I yield my soul in......

molto rit. - -

bliss!.....................

bliss!.....................

a tempo

(shouting)

La la la la la la la la! Tra

ff Orchestra

The Count applauds, then turns to the two young men   The Ladies slip away into their cabinets.

The Count applauds

rit. -   -   -   - a tempo

ff

la la la la la la la la la la

Bra - va! Bra-

94

The Musicians bow and take their leave. Bellina follows and draws the balcony curtains.

-vis-si-ma! Ex-cel-len-tis-si-ma! Bra-va! Bra-vis-si-ma!

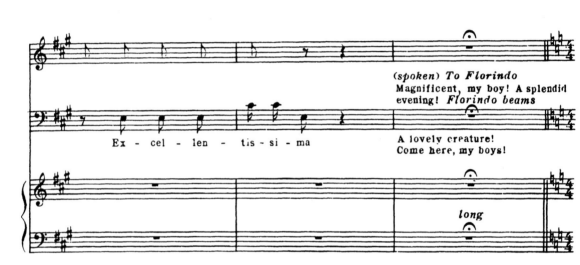

(spoken) To Florindo
Magnificent, my boy! A splendid evening! *Florindo beams*

Ex-cel-len-tis-si-ma

A lovely creature!
Come here, my boys!

long

The Count whispers to Florinda and Alcino who express the utmost consternation. The Count turns and finds no ladies.

Allegro molto

ALCINO

Why where is the girl? She has re-tired, Sir. She is—er— very shy.

H. 14184

Commodo quasi sopra

COUNT

Shy! La Fi-lo-me-la! Not if re- port speaks true! Go send he to me, boy.

It is my plea-sure she should come to me, And I can pay for my pleasures.

FLORINDO

Dear Sir, do you think it is wise? She has a

F4

FLOR.

ALCINO

friend— the Con- te Giu-lio—And he is as jea - lous as a fiend! Dear Sir, think

FLORINDO (*spoken*)
I tremble for
your safety should
it be known.

COUNT

ALC. twice be - fore you woo her.

My safe-ty? It's your

Allegro

OUNT own skin you fear for. Bah! Let your Con-te come and all his bra-vos!

F5

I'm not too old to meet him with my sword. You young-sters now-a-days are

cow - ards and weak-lings! God's life! No co-ward shall be heir of

(*ad lib:*)

H. 14184

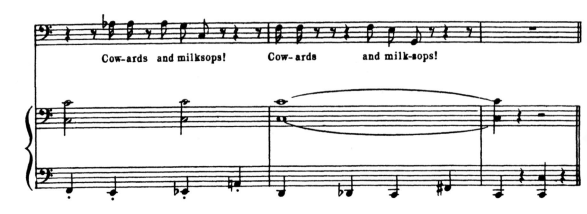

Cow-ards and milksops! Cow-ards and milk-sops!

The Count goes out left, grumbling to himself.
Alcino and Florindo sink into chairs

FLORINDO: And now?
ALCINO: And now? Why we must try to move them
And make one of them meet your Uncle's wish.
FLORINDO: One— yes, and only one this time,
Else all is lost.
Come, we can only try

long

They go up to the Cabinets and try the handles of the doors
which they find locked. They knock.

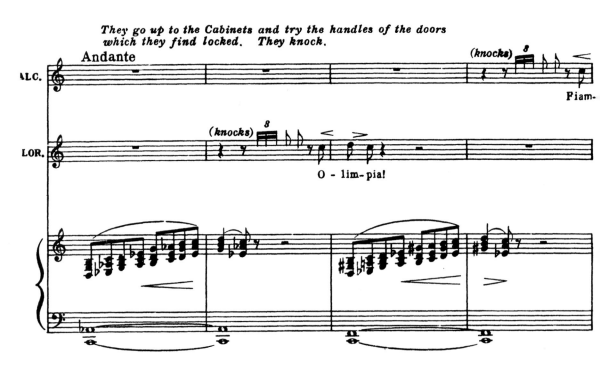

O - lim-pia!

They listen. There is no sound.
They come down disconsolately

FLORINDO (*spoken*) Only one hope remains. Some way or other we must win their pity.

Florindo produces two pistols. He then speaks in a low voice to Alcino.

— met - ta!   I im - plore   you!

(knocks) I be-seech you!

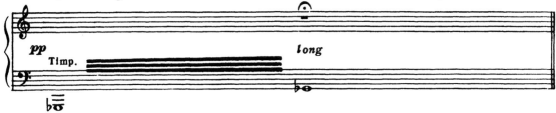

FLORINDO (*spoken*) Take this and fire it into the air. Then lie down and pretend to be dead.

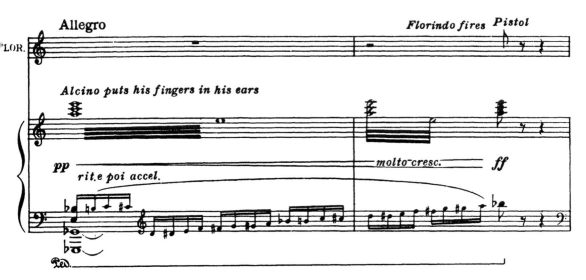

Allegro

Florindo fires Pistol

Alcino puts his fingers in his ears

H. 14184

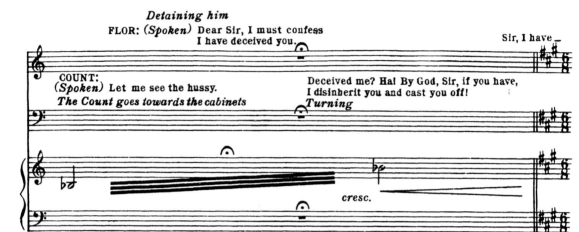

Detaining him
FLOR: *(Spoken)* Dear Sir, I must confess
I have deceived you.

COUNT:
(Spoken) Let me see the hussy.
The Count goes towards the cabinets

Deceived me? Ha! By God, Sir, if you have,
I disinherit you and cast you off!
Turning

Sir, I have ___

Suddenly the curtains are drawn apart and Bellina appears in one of the "Ariadne" dresses. All turn and stare at her.

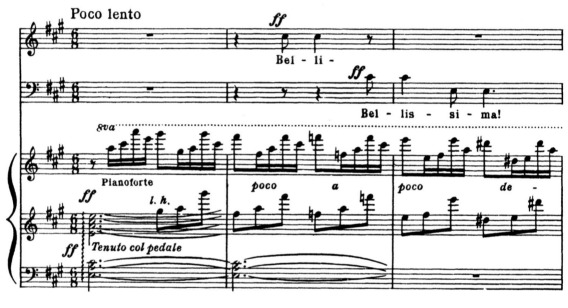

Poco lento

Bel - li -

Bel - lis - si - ma!

Pianoforte
l. h.

poco   a   poco   de -

Tenuto col pedale

G7

She courtseys to the Count

BELL.

La Fi - lo - me - la,   at your

- cres - cen - do

BELL.
ser - vice, Sir.

COUNT
Was this your de-cep-tion, rogue?

The Count

FLOR.
A little jest, Sir.   Pardon me, I   beg!

henceforth has eyes for none except Bellina. He leads her to the couch.

F 10
dolcissimo

COUNT
Come,   bell-iss - - - i - ma,

Flt.

Come, my song - bird. We have had mu - sic,

We have had wine.
Clt.
What more remains to

fill our cup? To crown the trin-i-ty di - vine?........

G
Coyly — keeping out of his reach

BELL.
Oh, Sir!   Oh, Sir!

OUNT
Love .... on - ly Love!...........................

rit. - - - - - - - - attacca

During the following scene Alcino and Florindo steal to the back and quietly knock on the doors of the cabinets. After a while the two Ladies come out in their ordinary dresses. The two men plead with them; the Ladies gradually relent; and, as Bellina yields to the Count, are reconciled to the men. Eventually the Ladies embrace each other. All four then retire to the cabinets in pairs.

The sky-lark wooed her the whole day long, Trilling his most me-lo - dious song. The

He hangs jewels on Bellina

OUNT

thrush offered worms pulled out of the earth, The mag-pie gems of the rar - est worth. But the

lit tle brown night-in-gale sat in her tree, And ne-ver a word to them all said

BELL.

tiou tiou tiou tiou tiou tiou-ee tiou - ee tiou-ee ah.............

OUNT

she...........

108

H. 14184

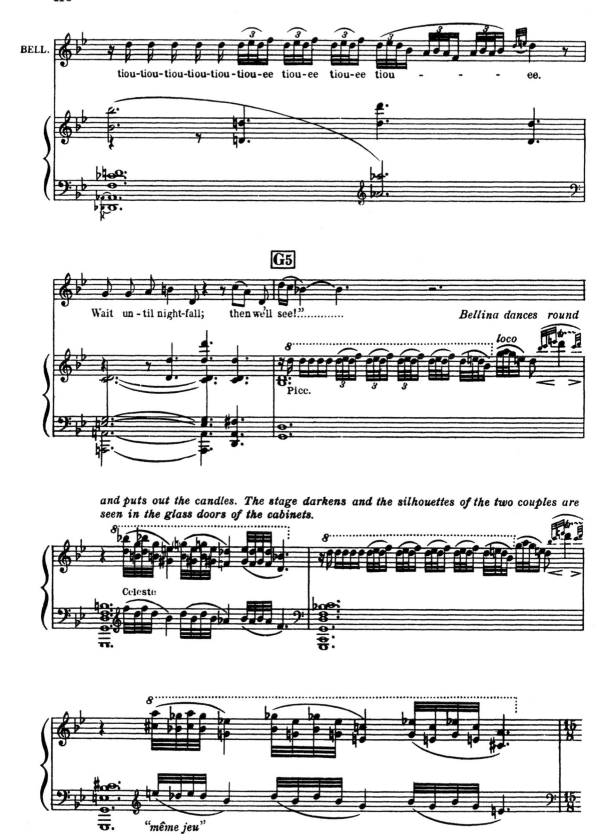

BELL.

tiou-tiou-tiou-tiou-tiou-tiou-ee tiou-ee tiou-ee tiou - - ee.

G5

Wait un-til night-fall; then we'll see!"............. *Bellina dances round*

loco

Picc.

and puts out the candles. The stage darkens and the silhouettes of the two couples are
seen in the glass doors of the cabinets.

Celeste

"même jeu"

G6

*The door of one cabinet opens slowly and
boots and a bandbox are placed outside.*

tiou-ee tiou-ee tiou-ee   tiou-ee

Quite maudlin falsetto

Tu-whit, tu-whoo!

The other door opens— "même jeu"

loco

The lights in the cabinets are extinguished and the room is lighted only by the moonlight –

loco

G7 Fl.

Pianoforte

l.h.

from the Canal as the Curtain slowly falls.

Clt.

Fine
Aug. 1933

H. 14184